MONSTERS

In The Mall

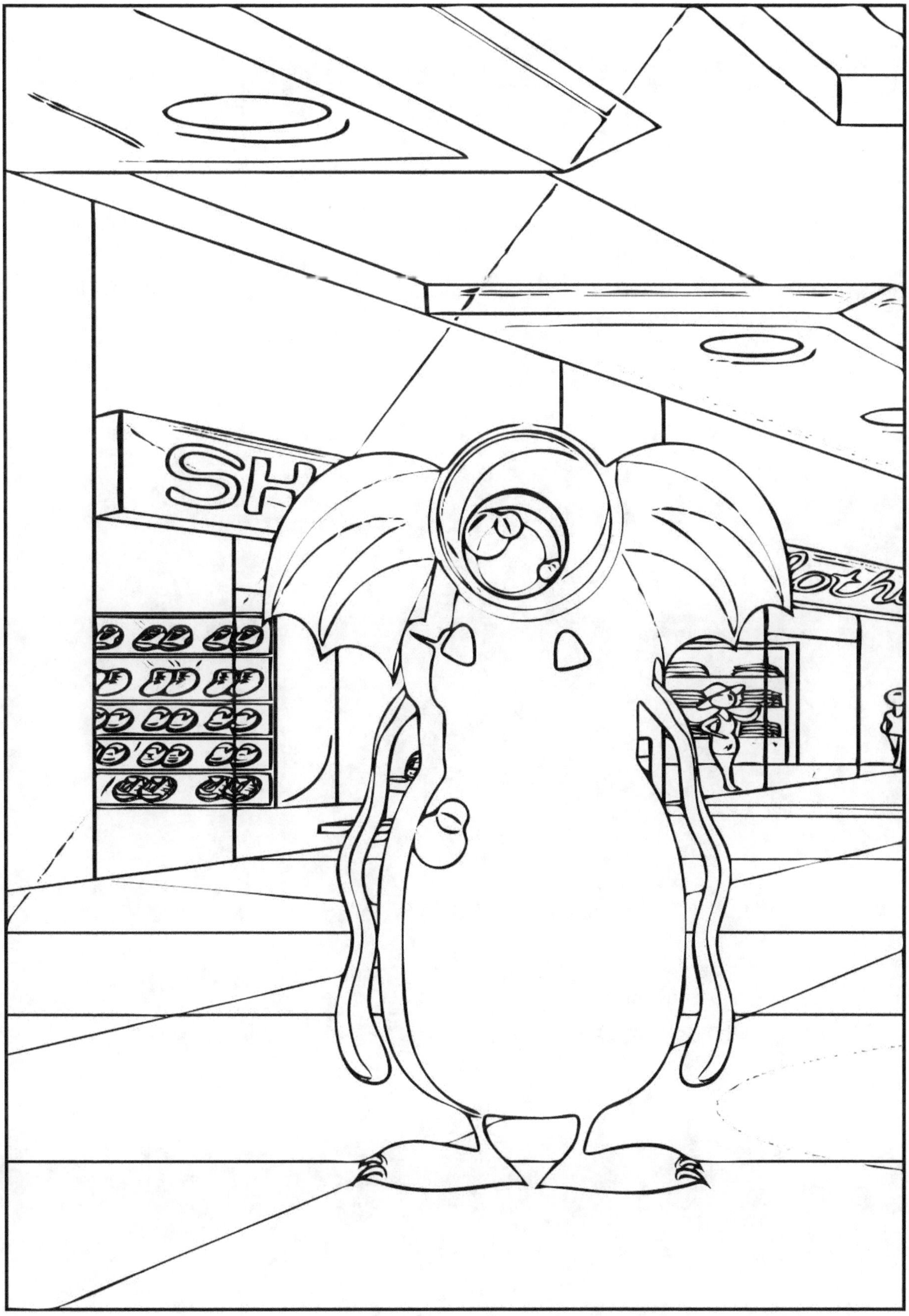
SH

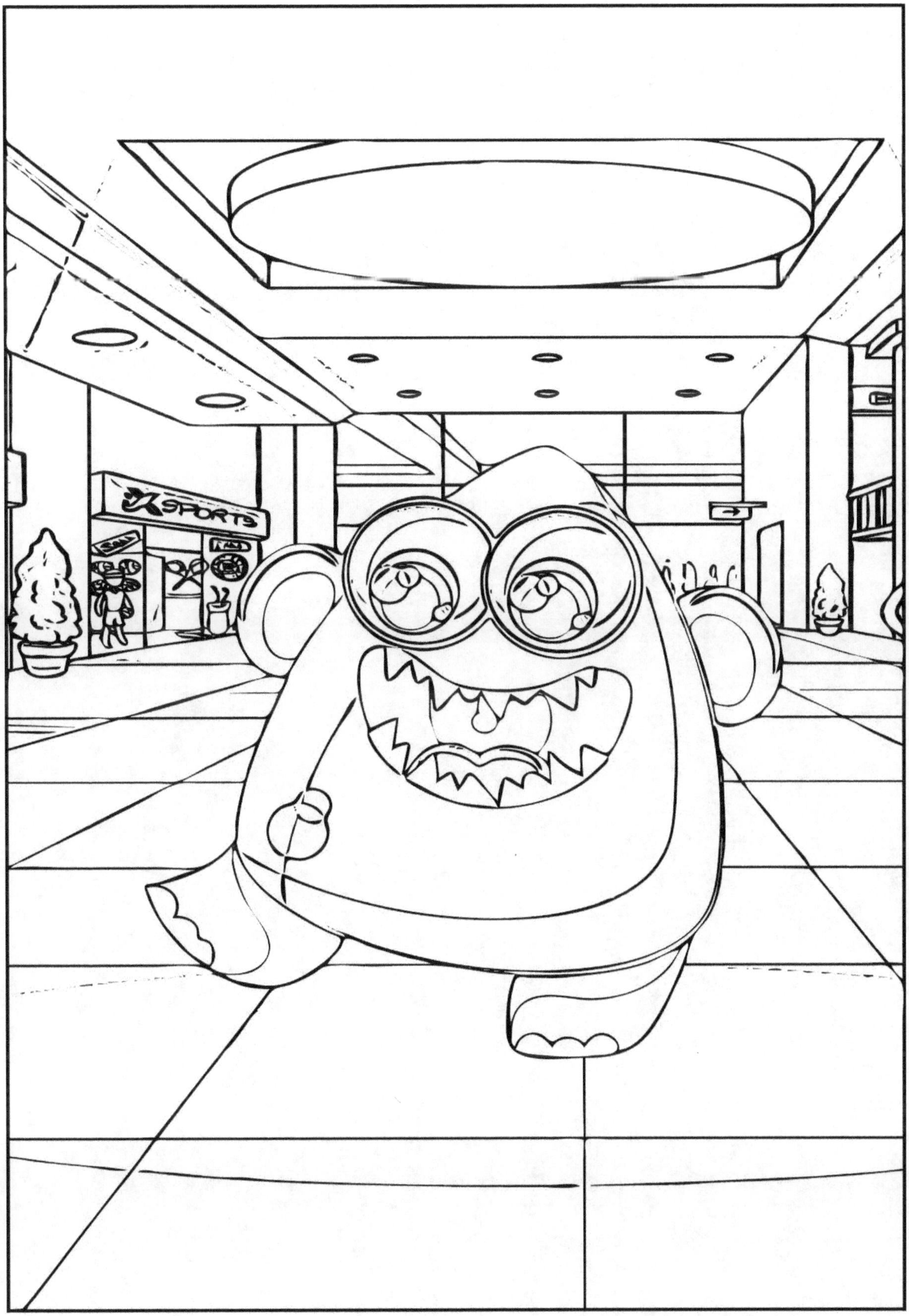
SPORTS

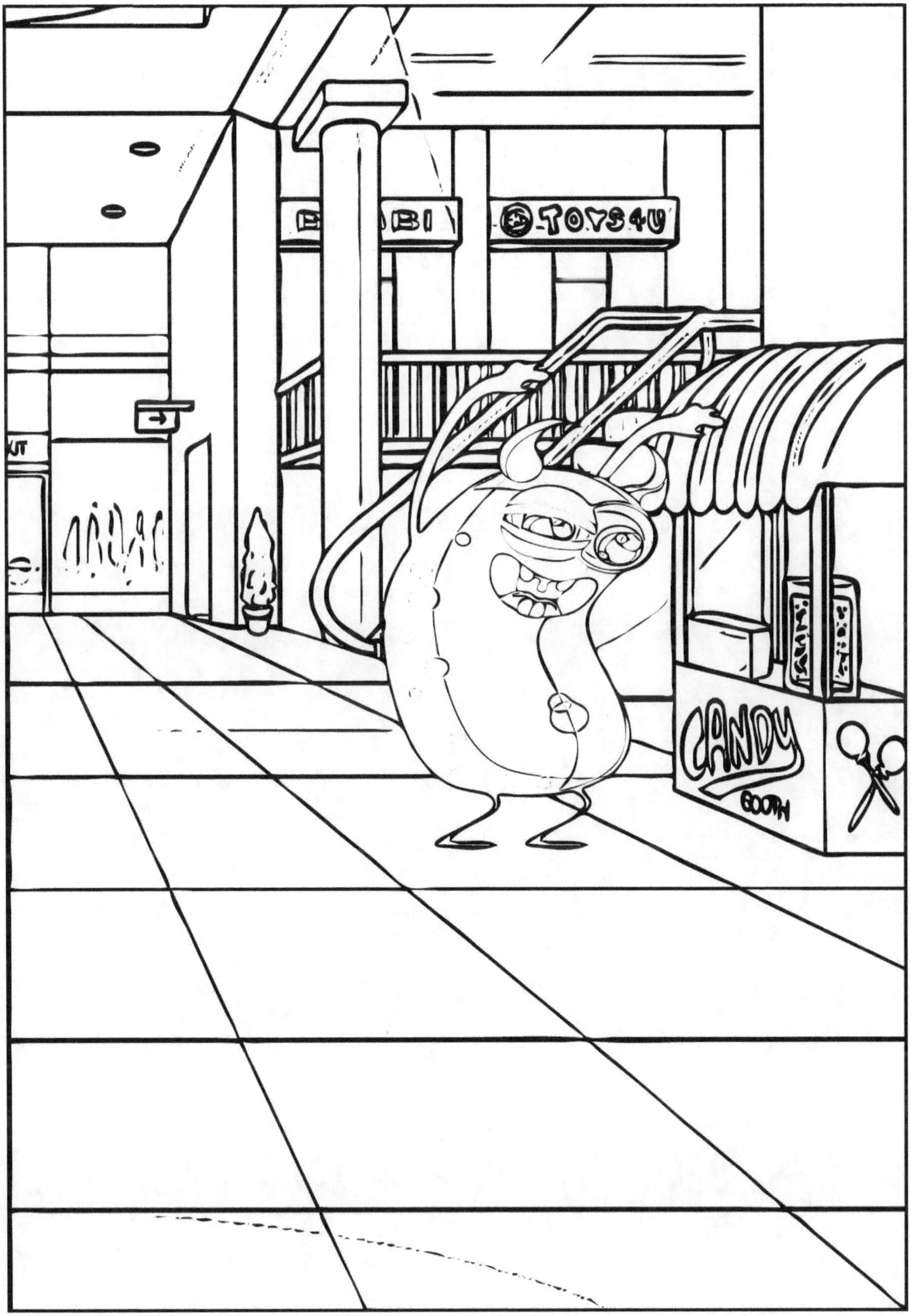
TOYS4U
CANDY
BOOTH

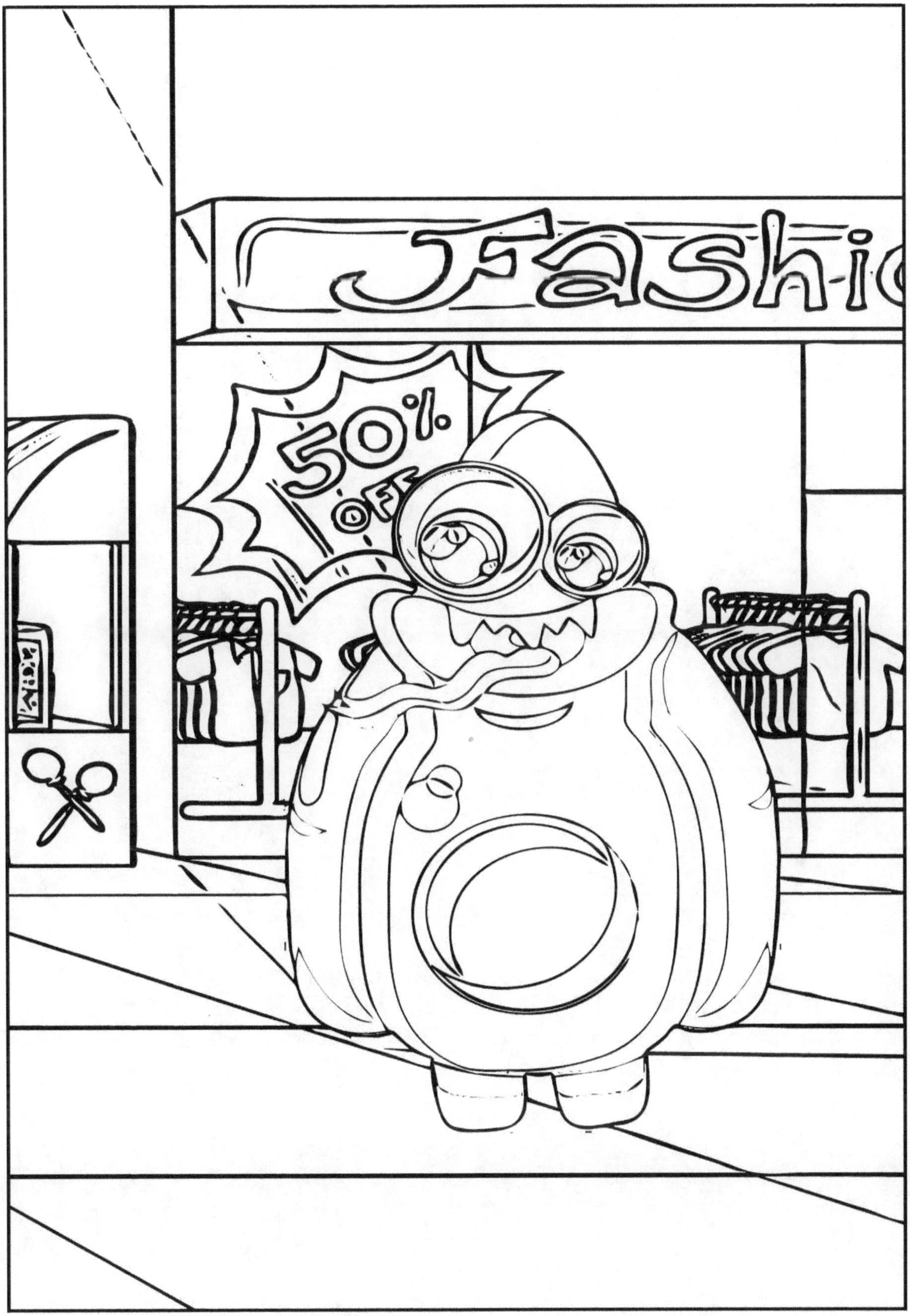
Fashio
50%
OFF

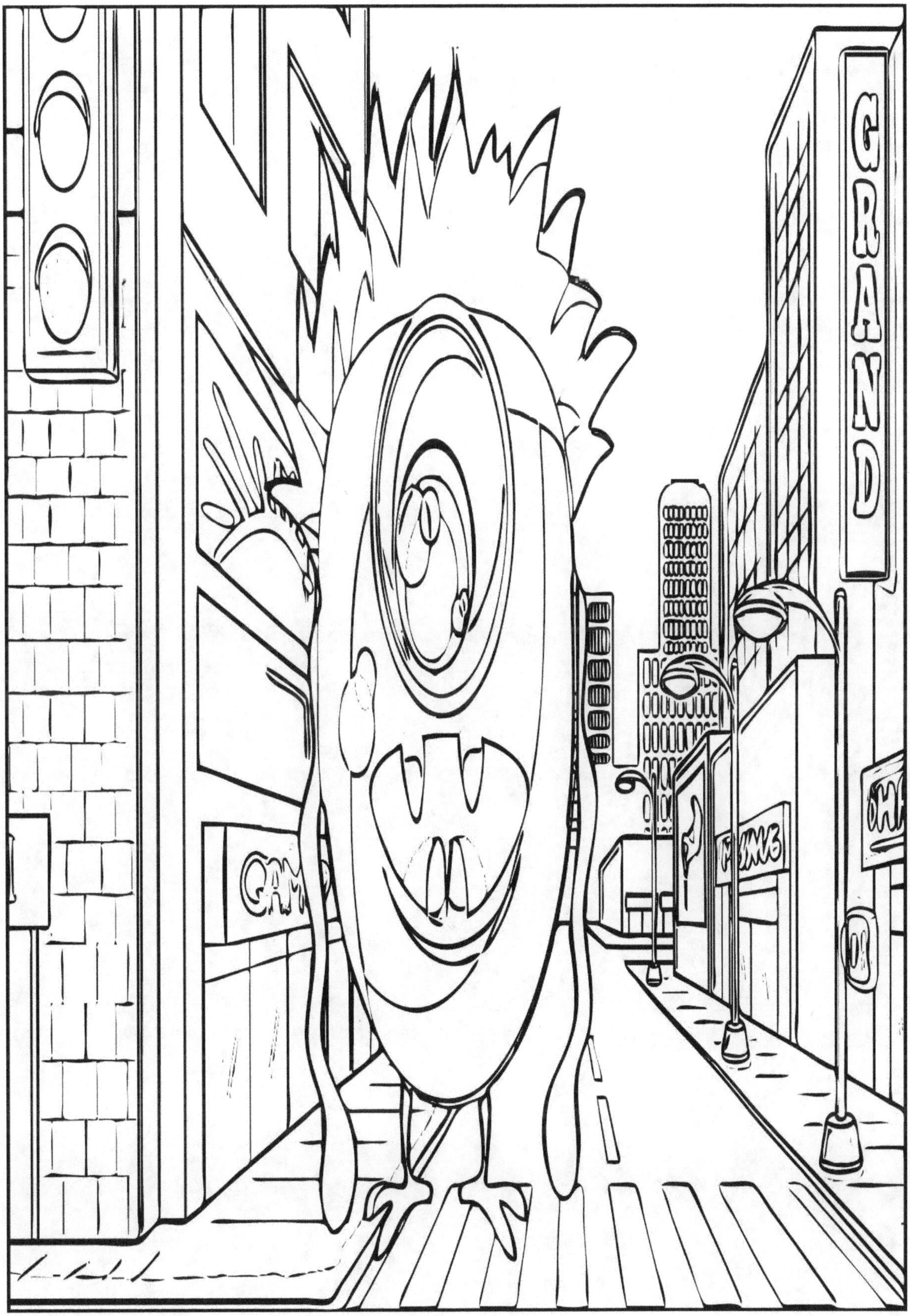
GRAND

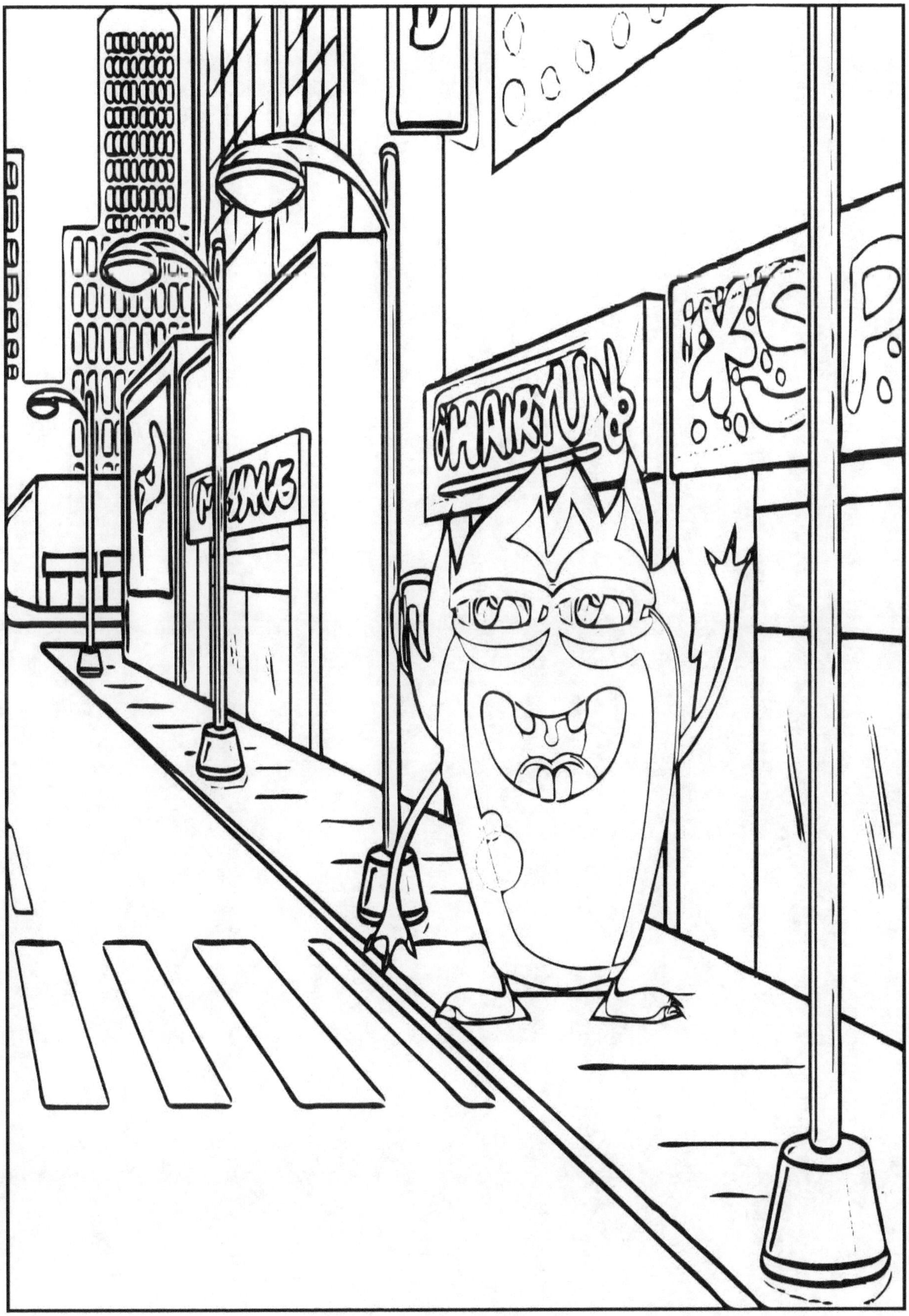
HAIRYU

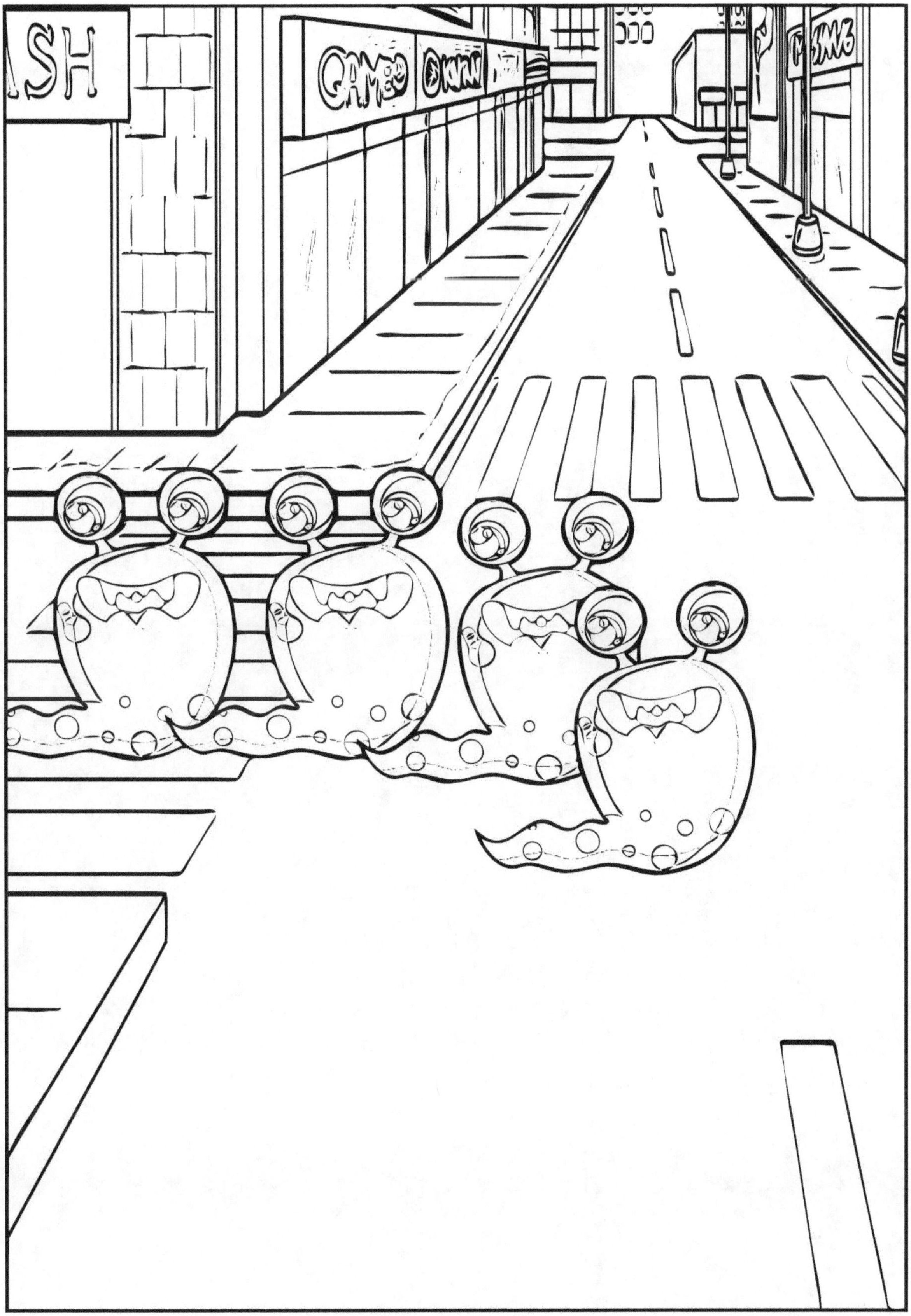
ASH

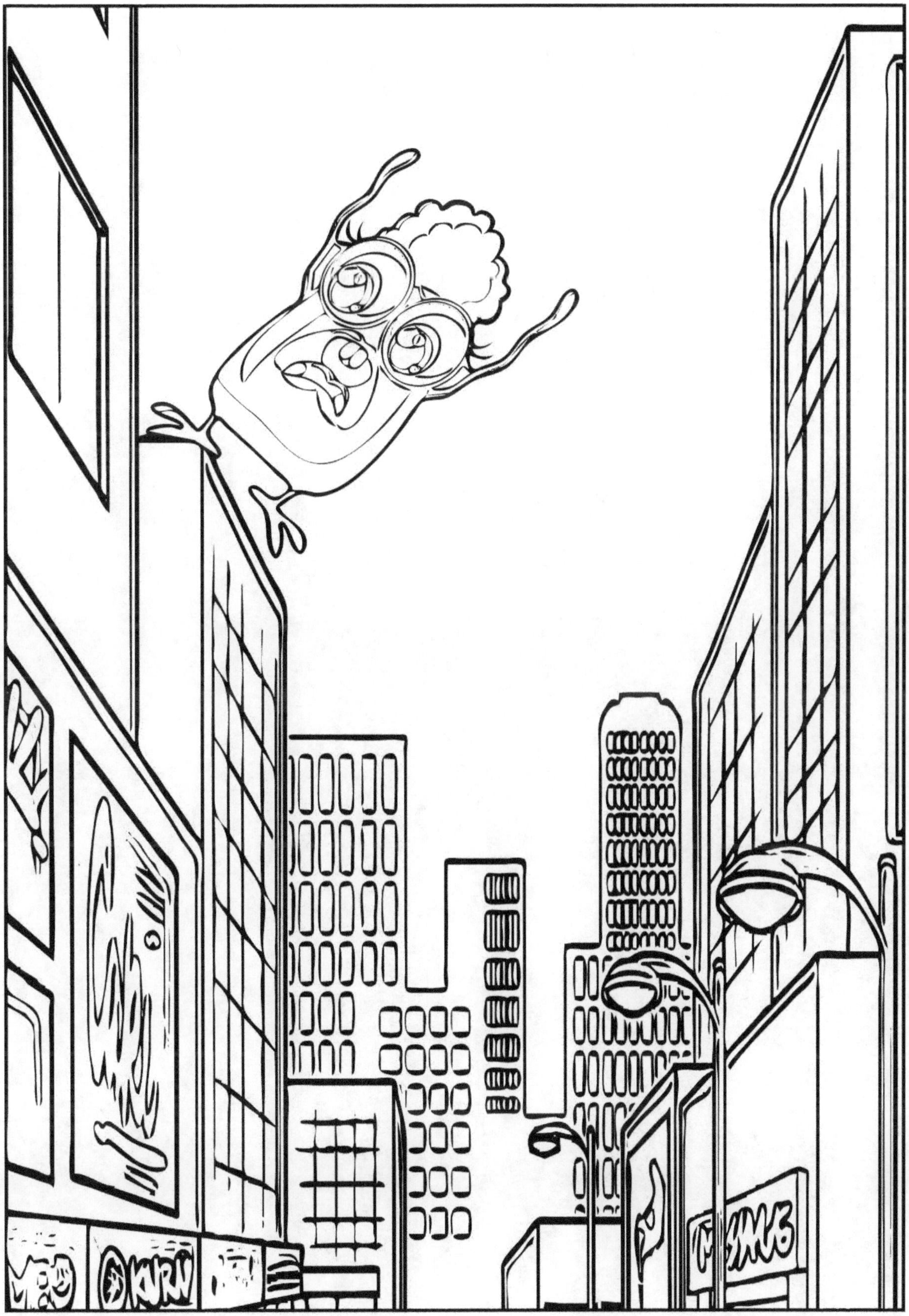

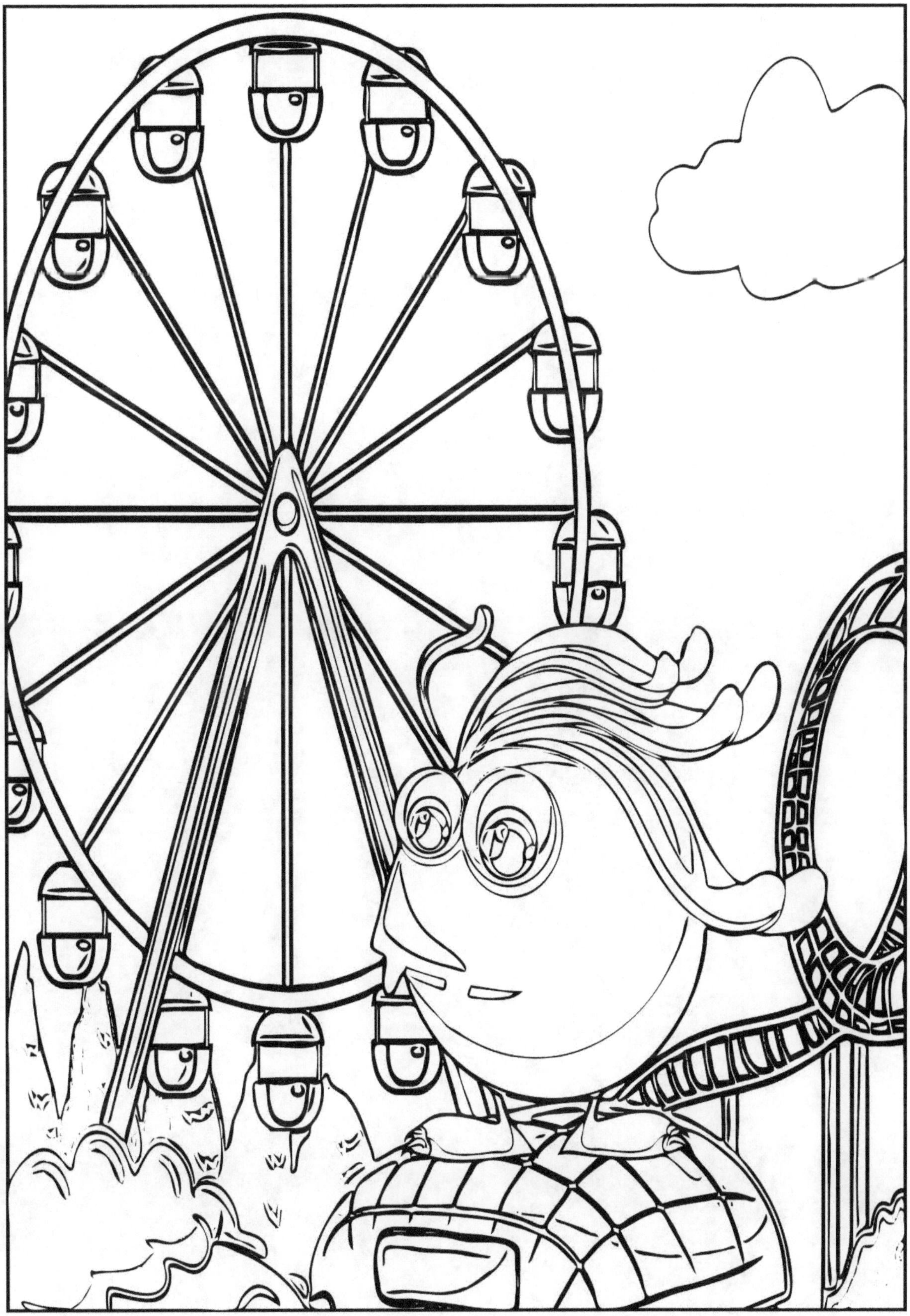

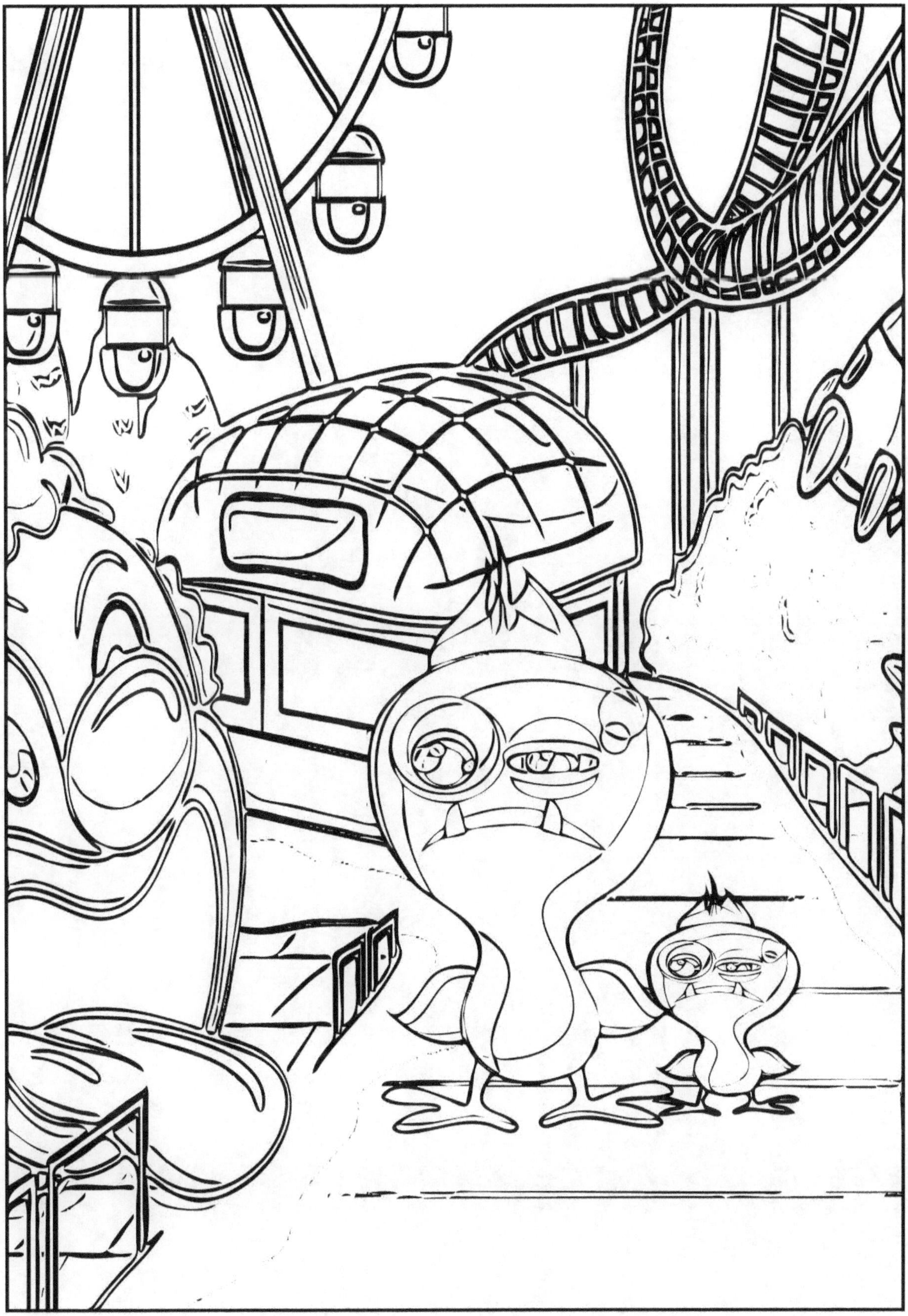

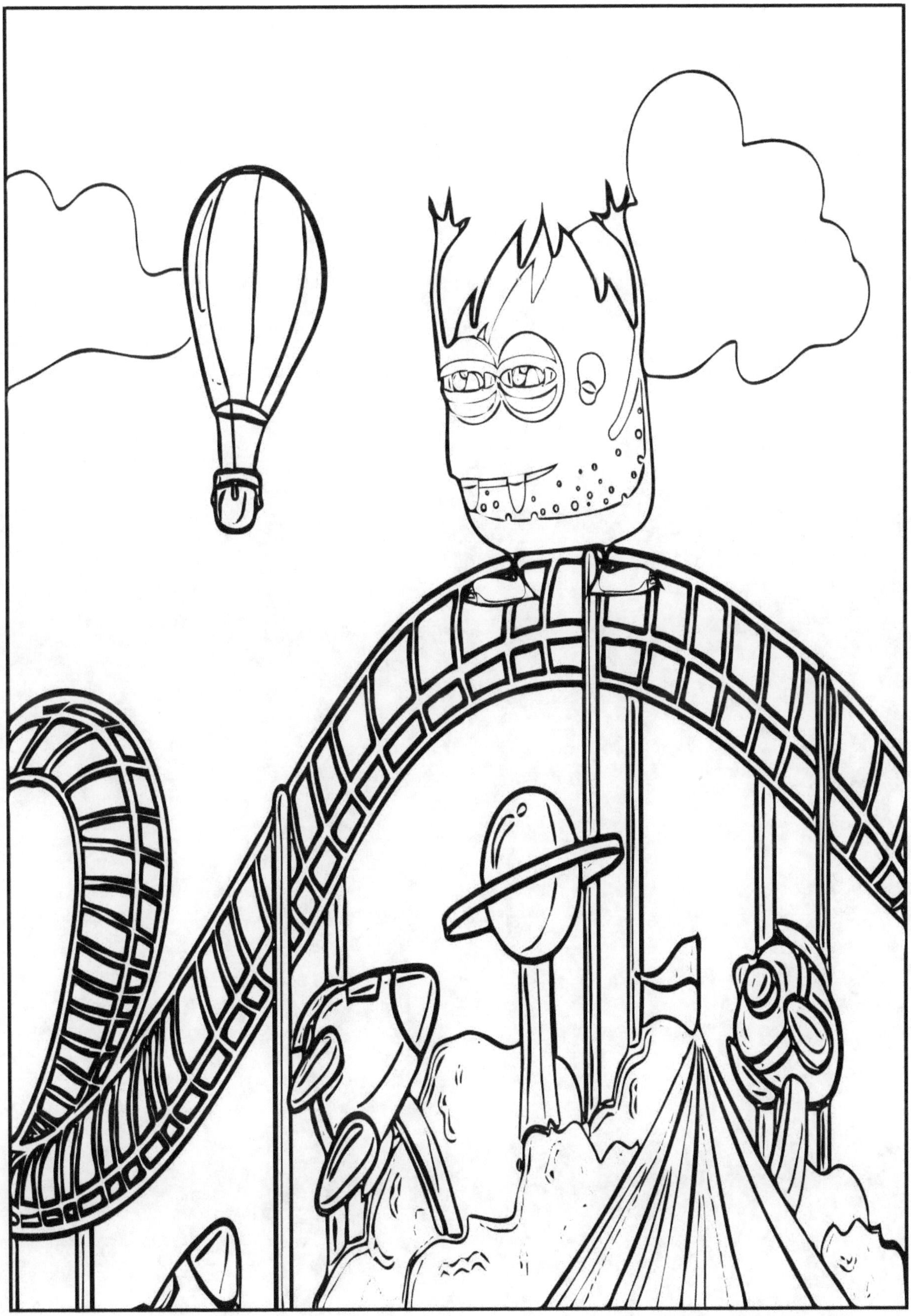

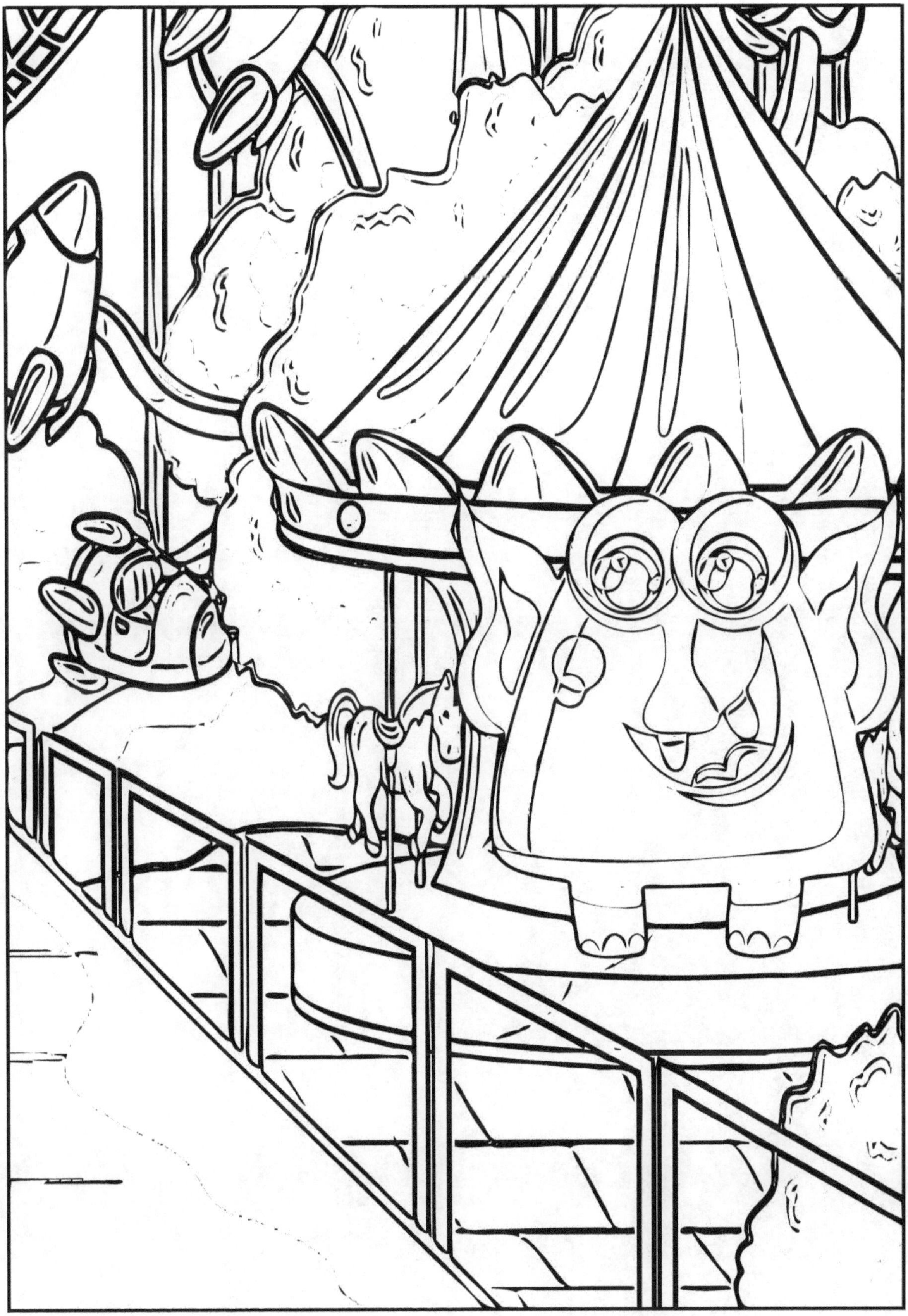

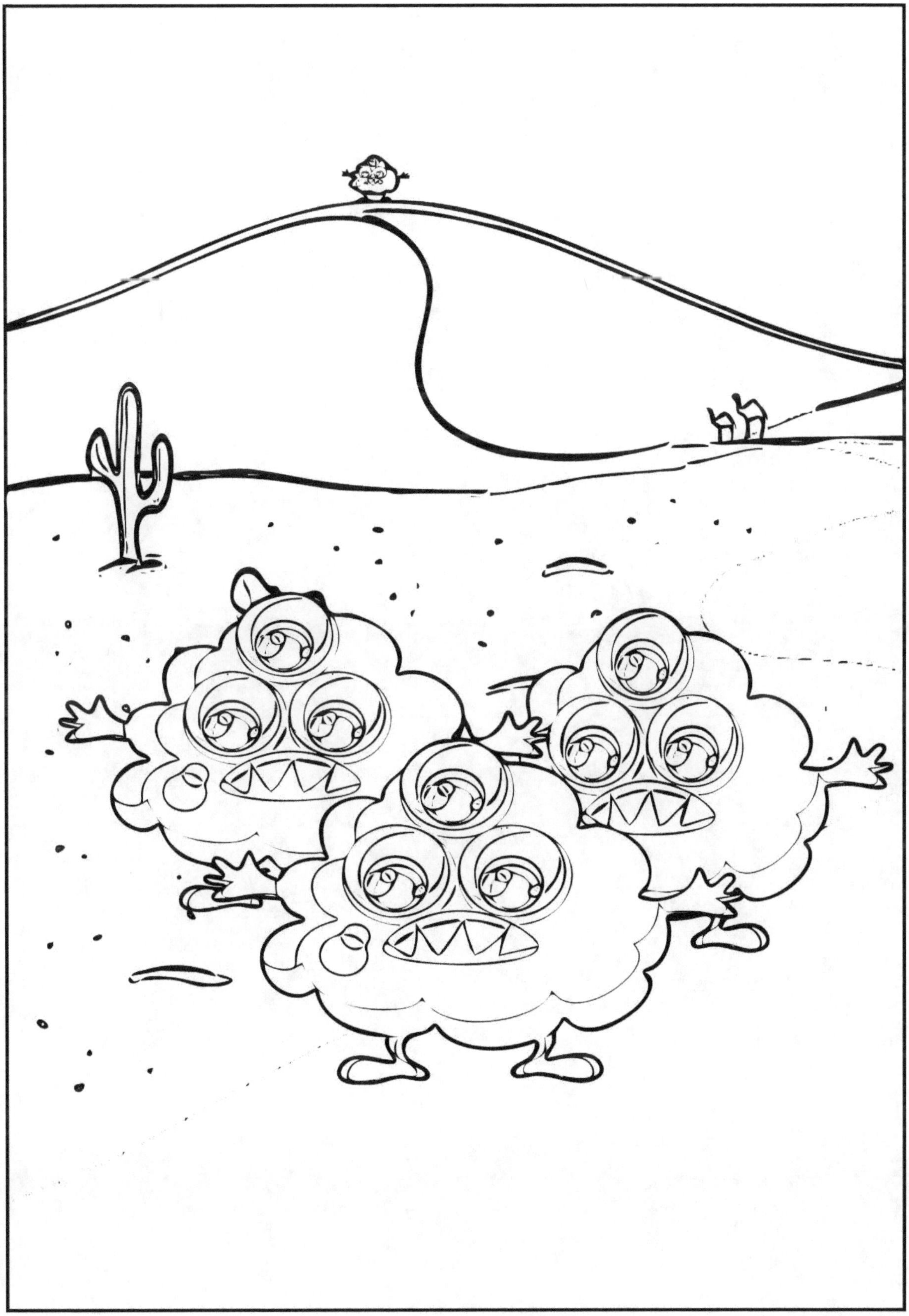

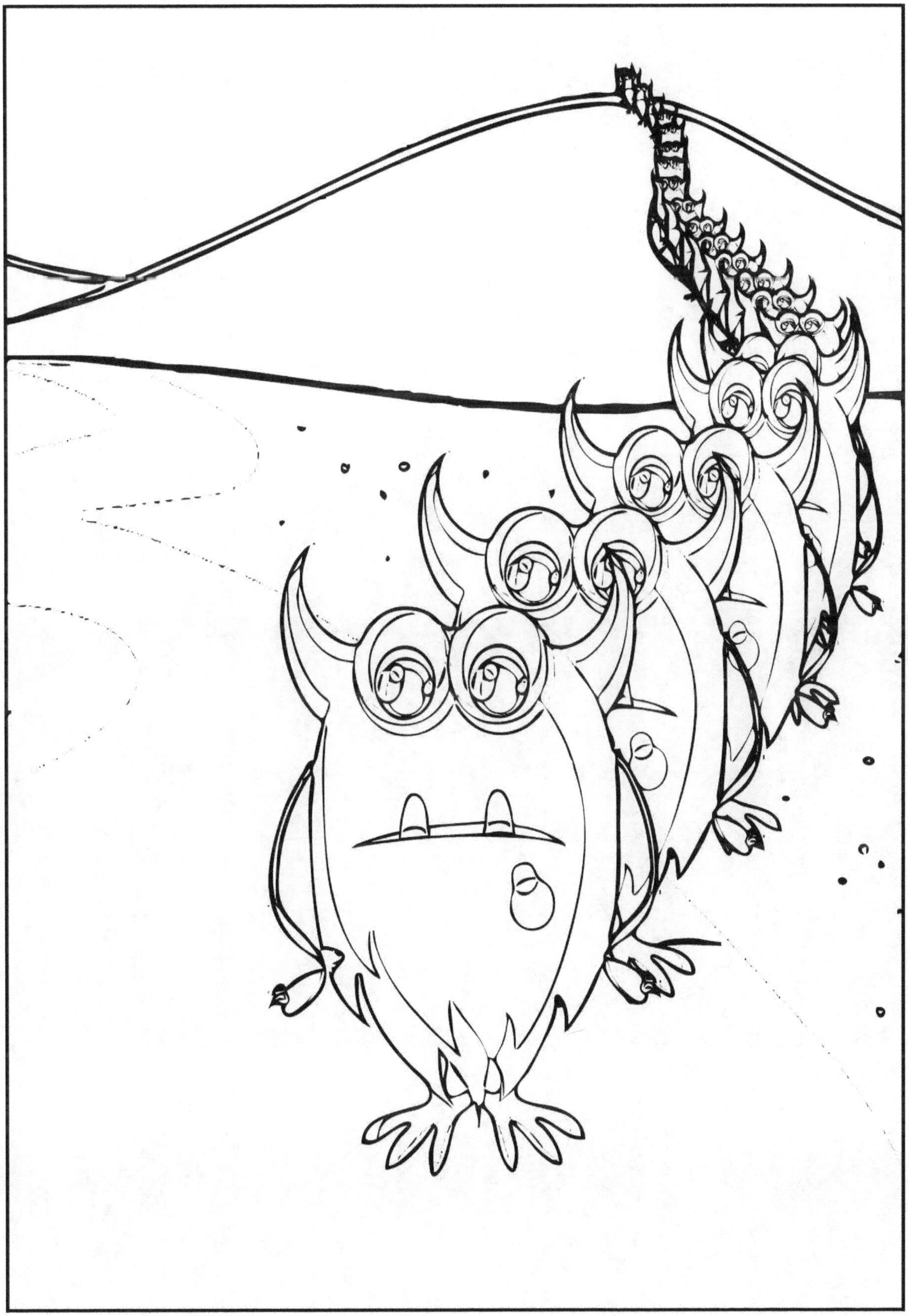

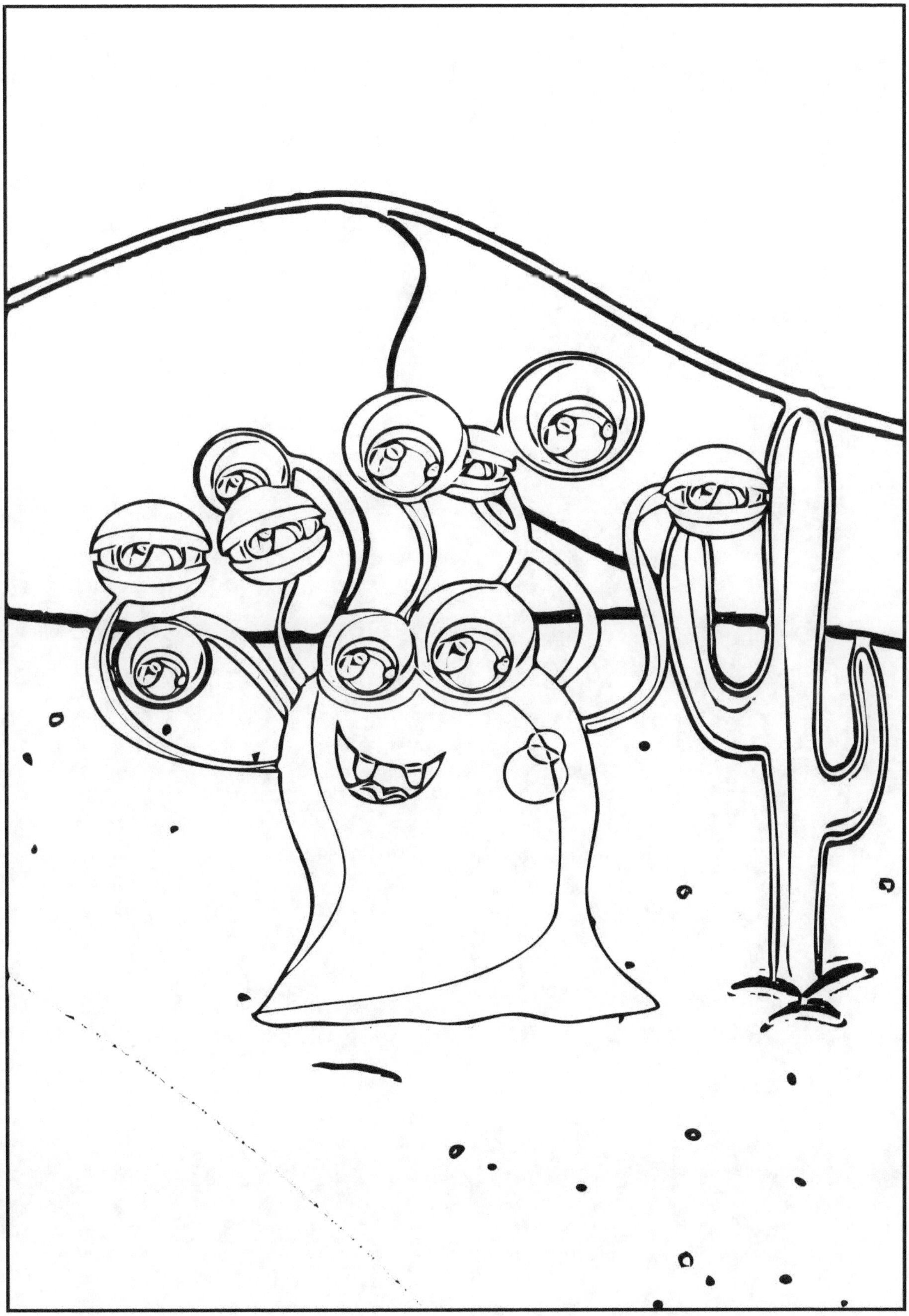

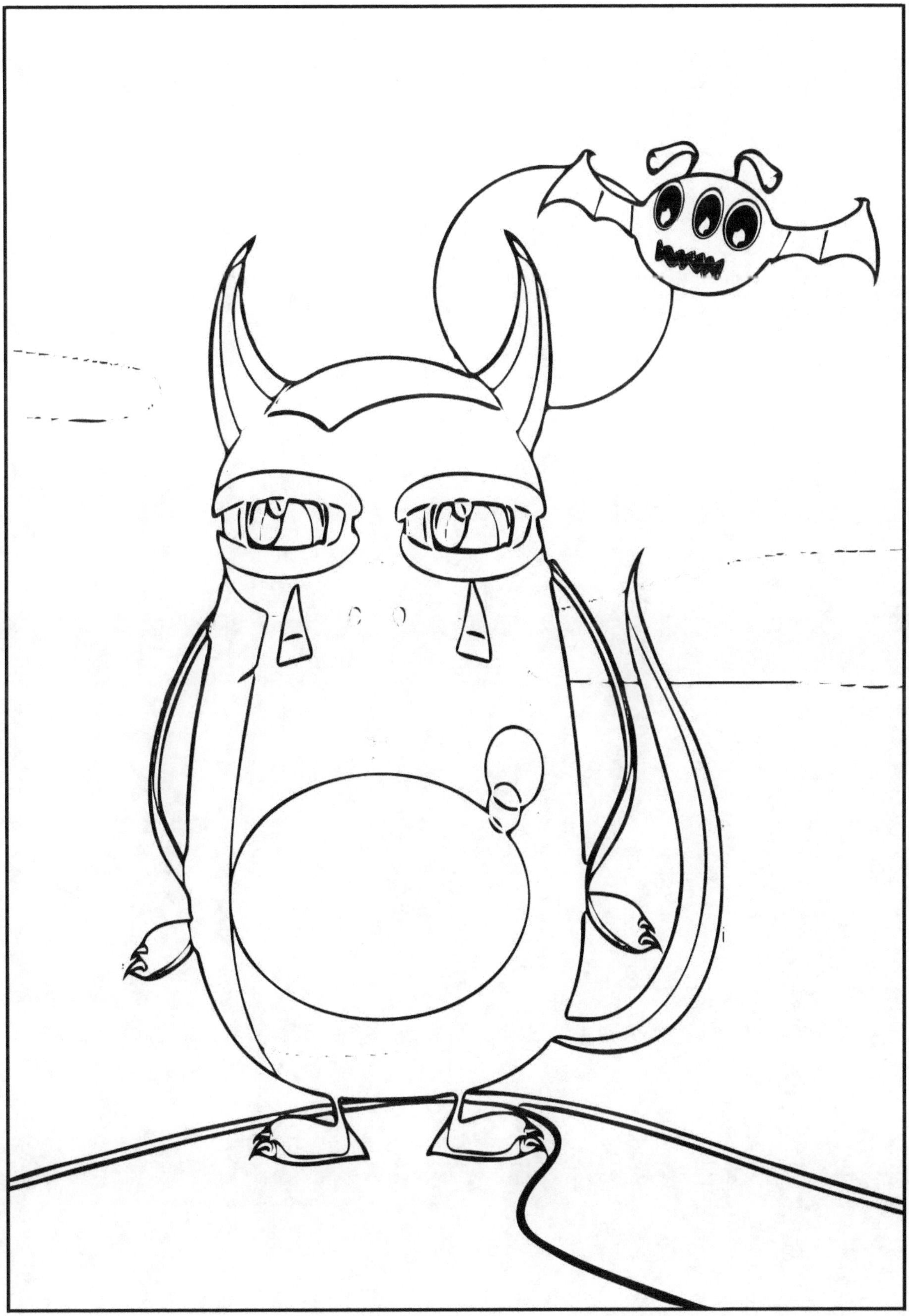

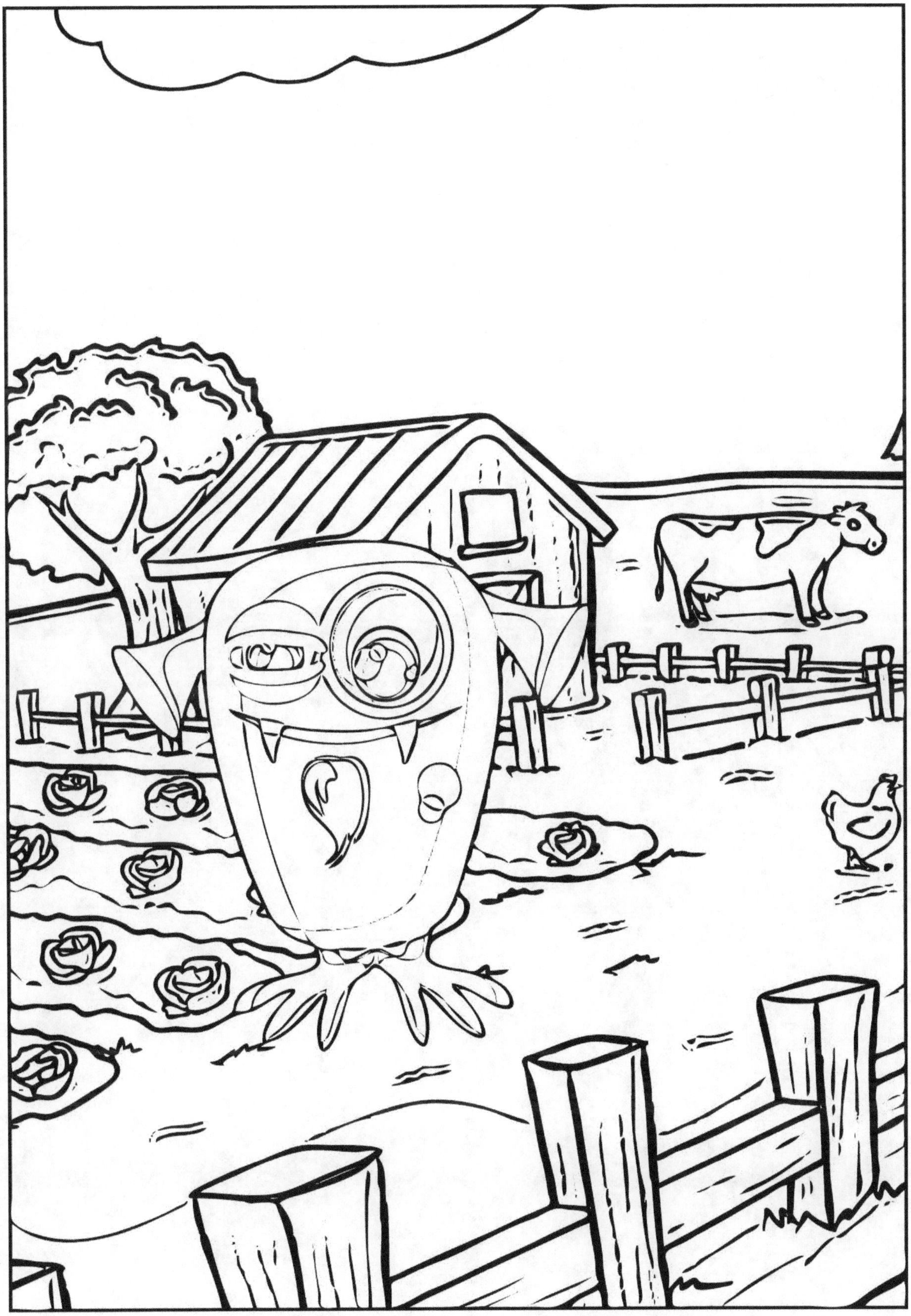

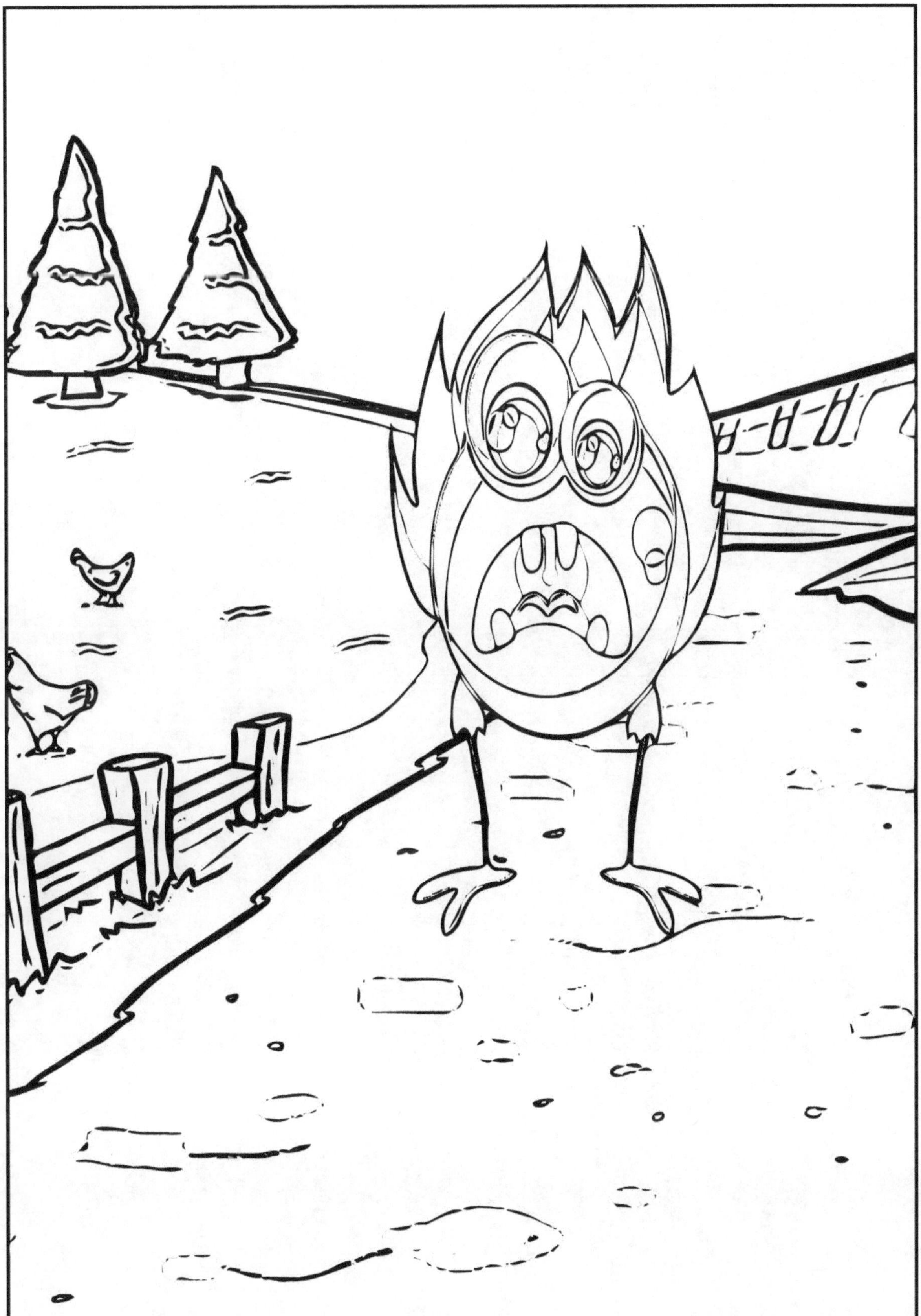

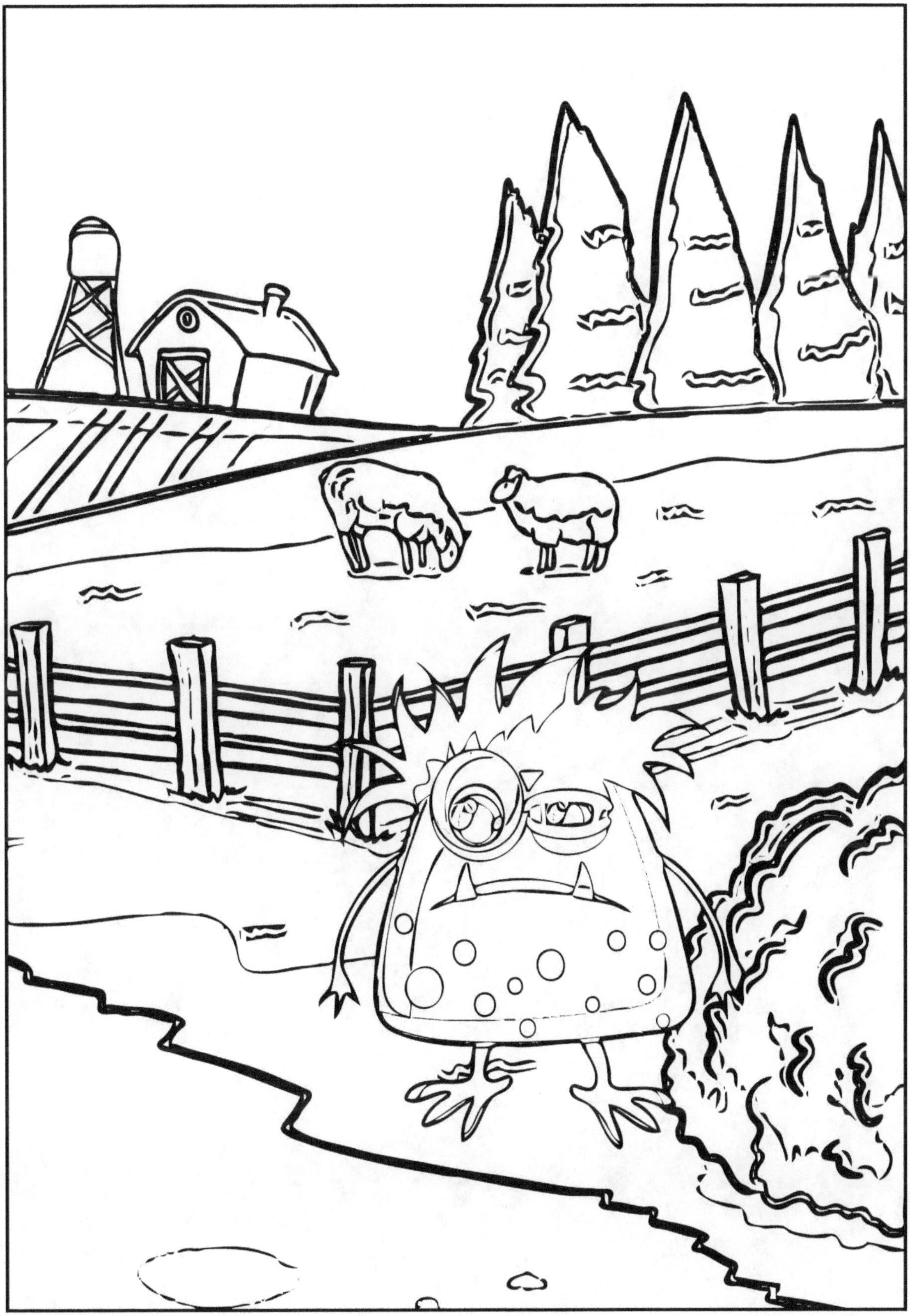

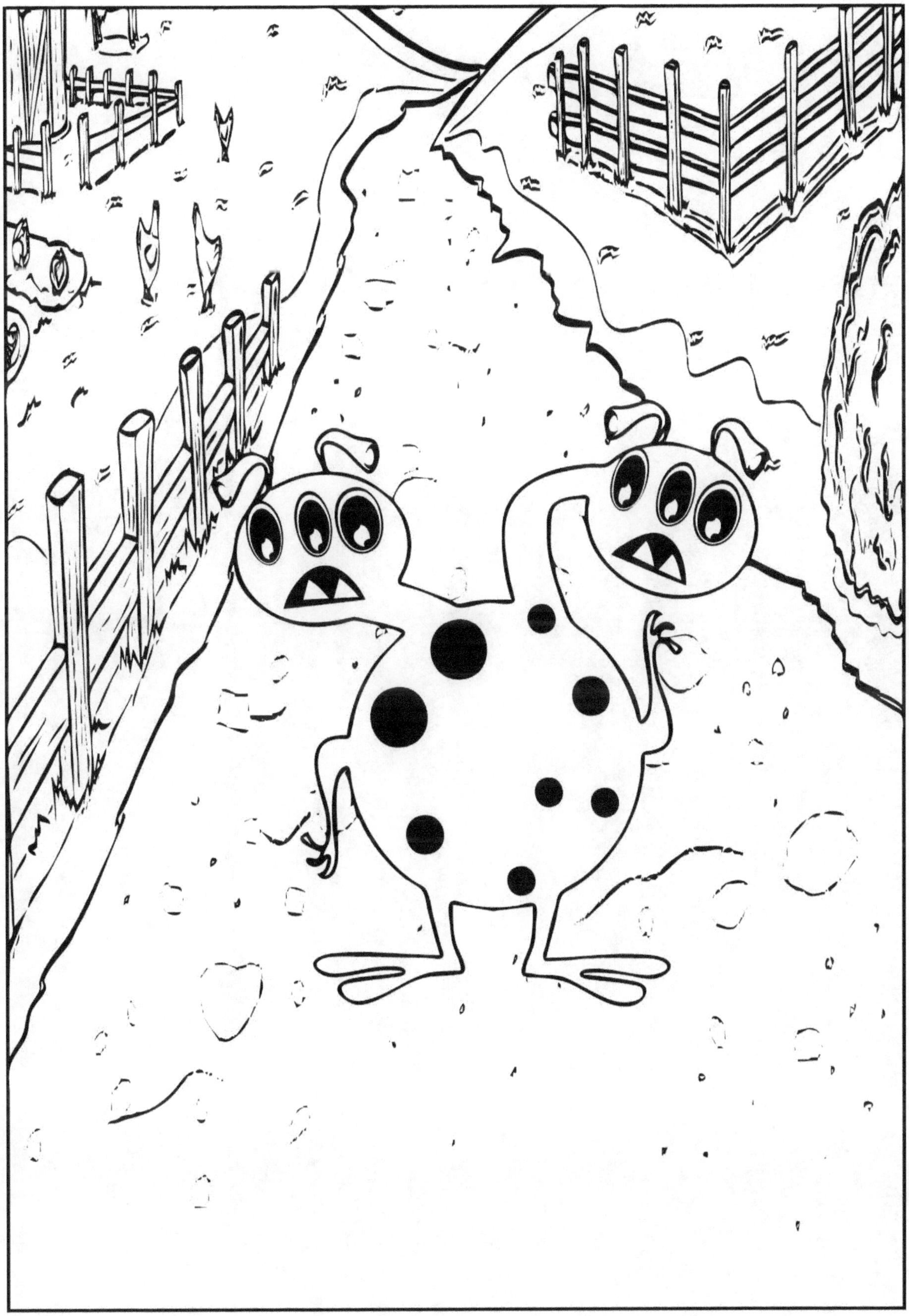

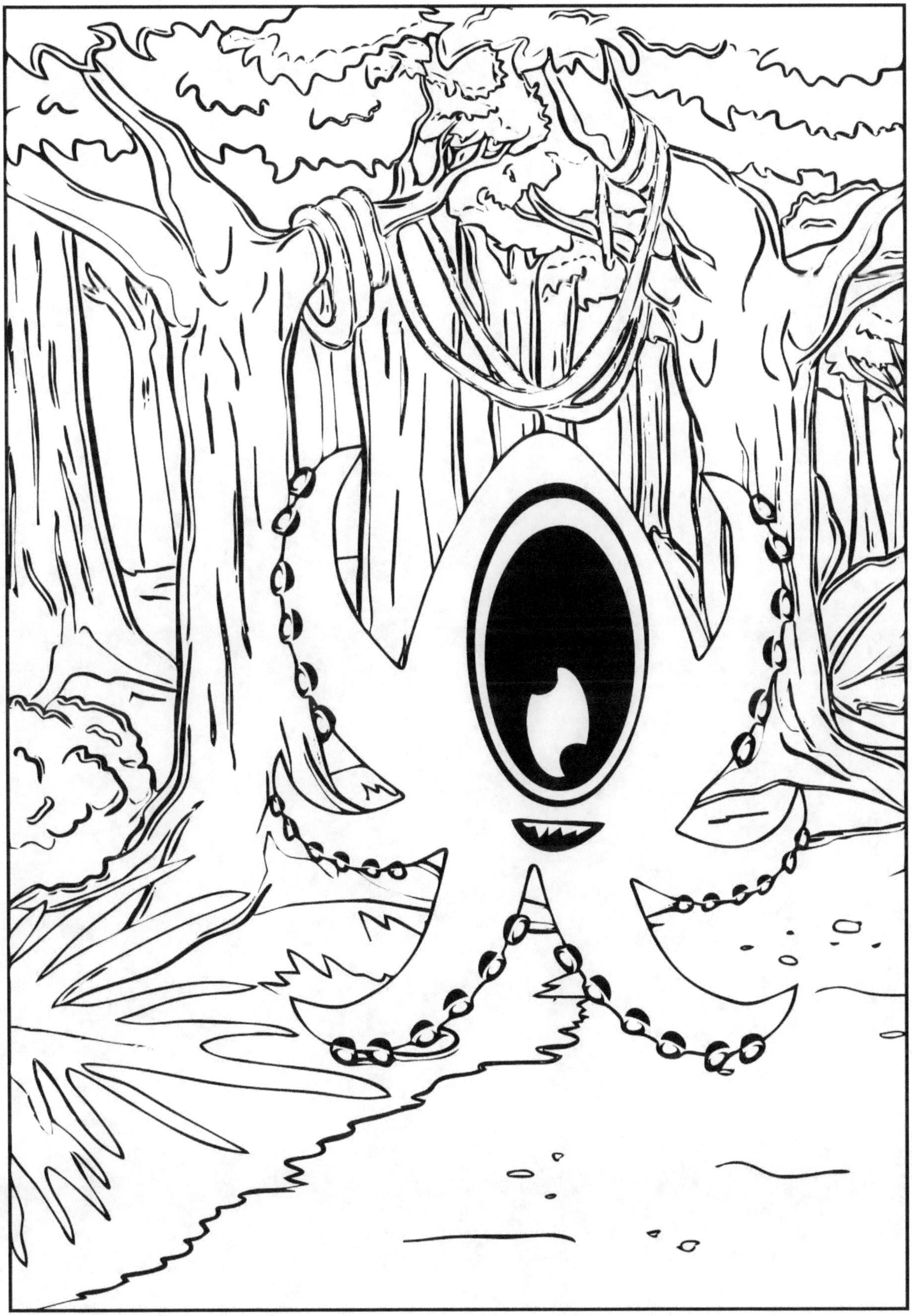

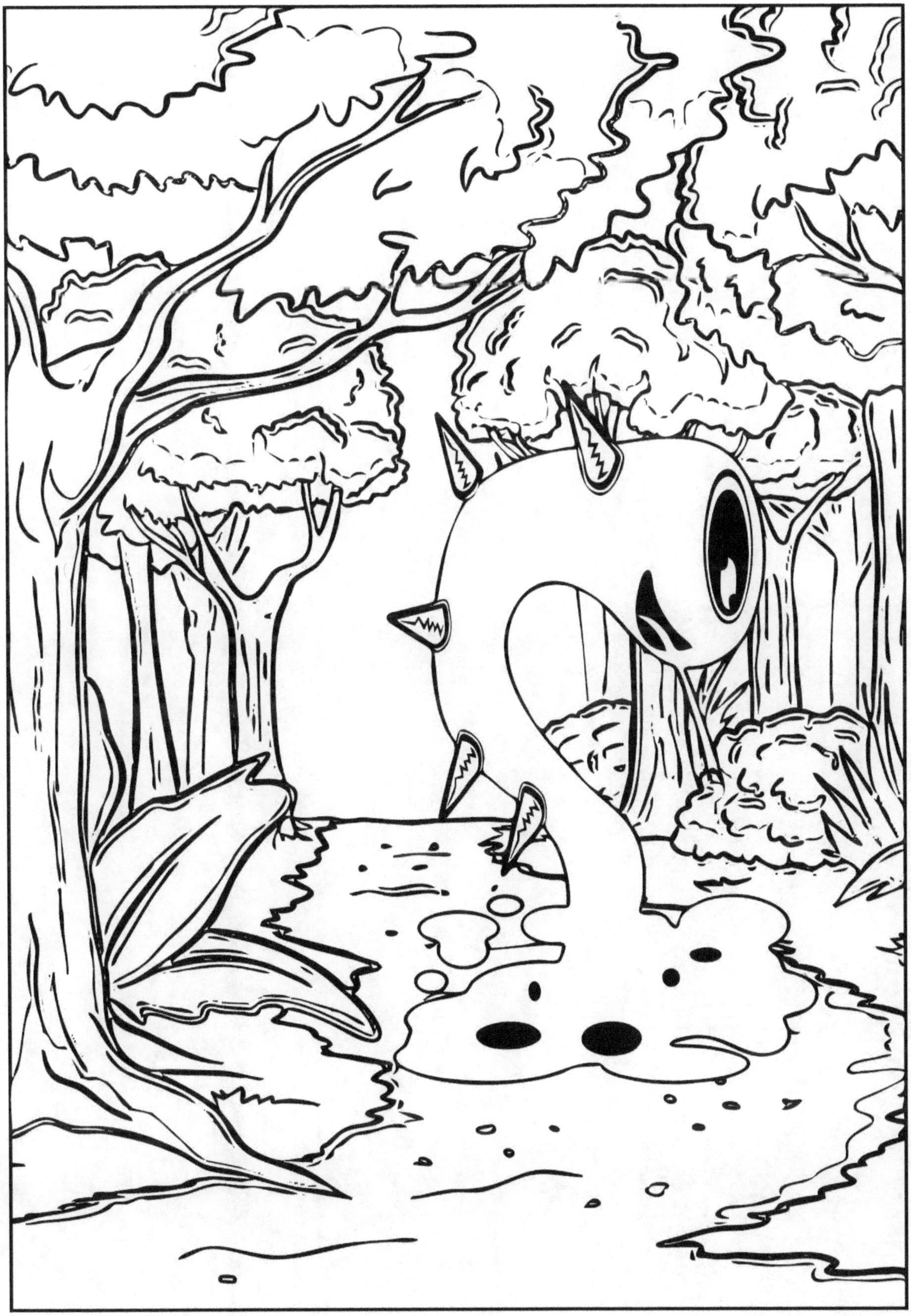

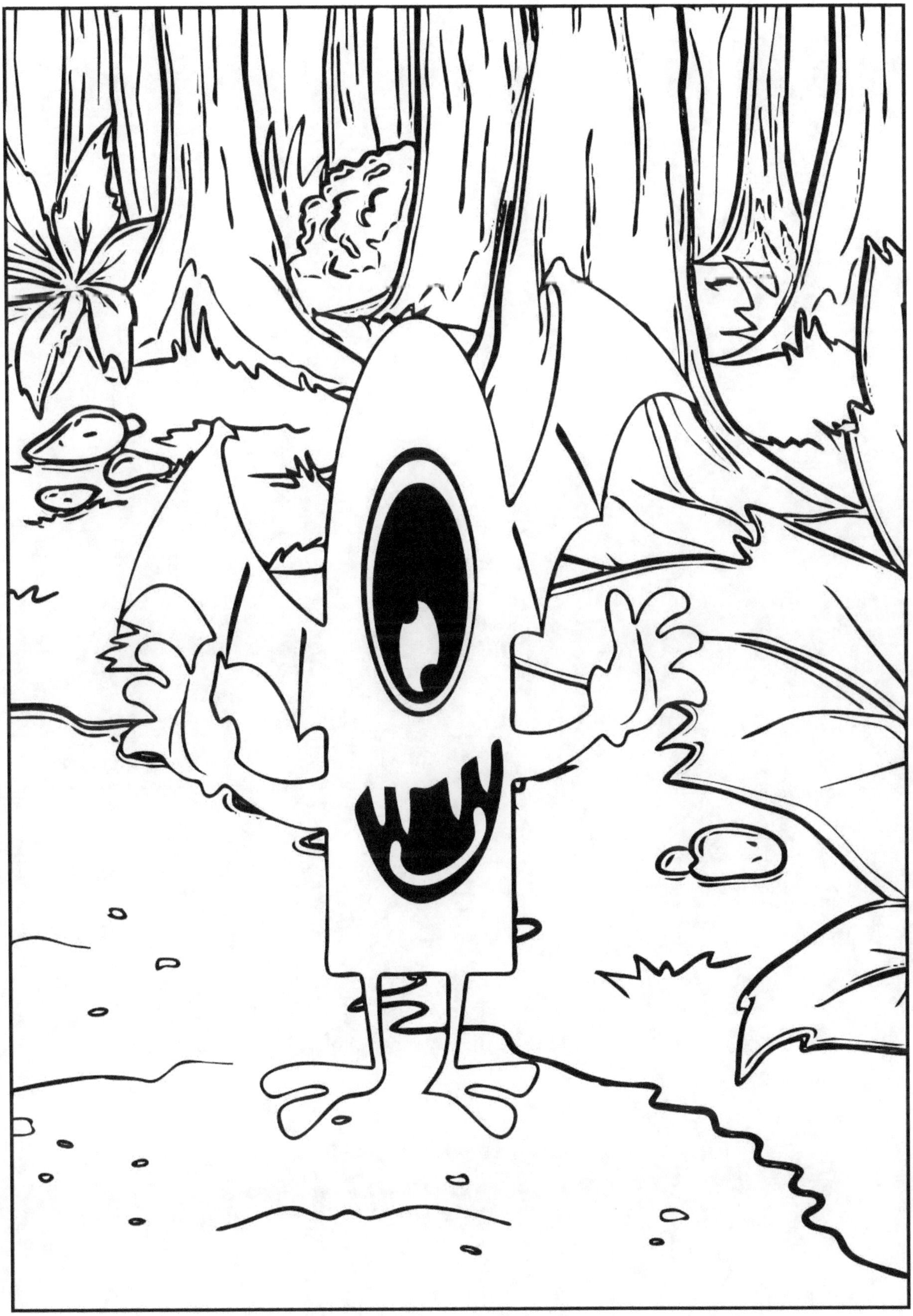

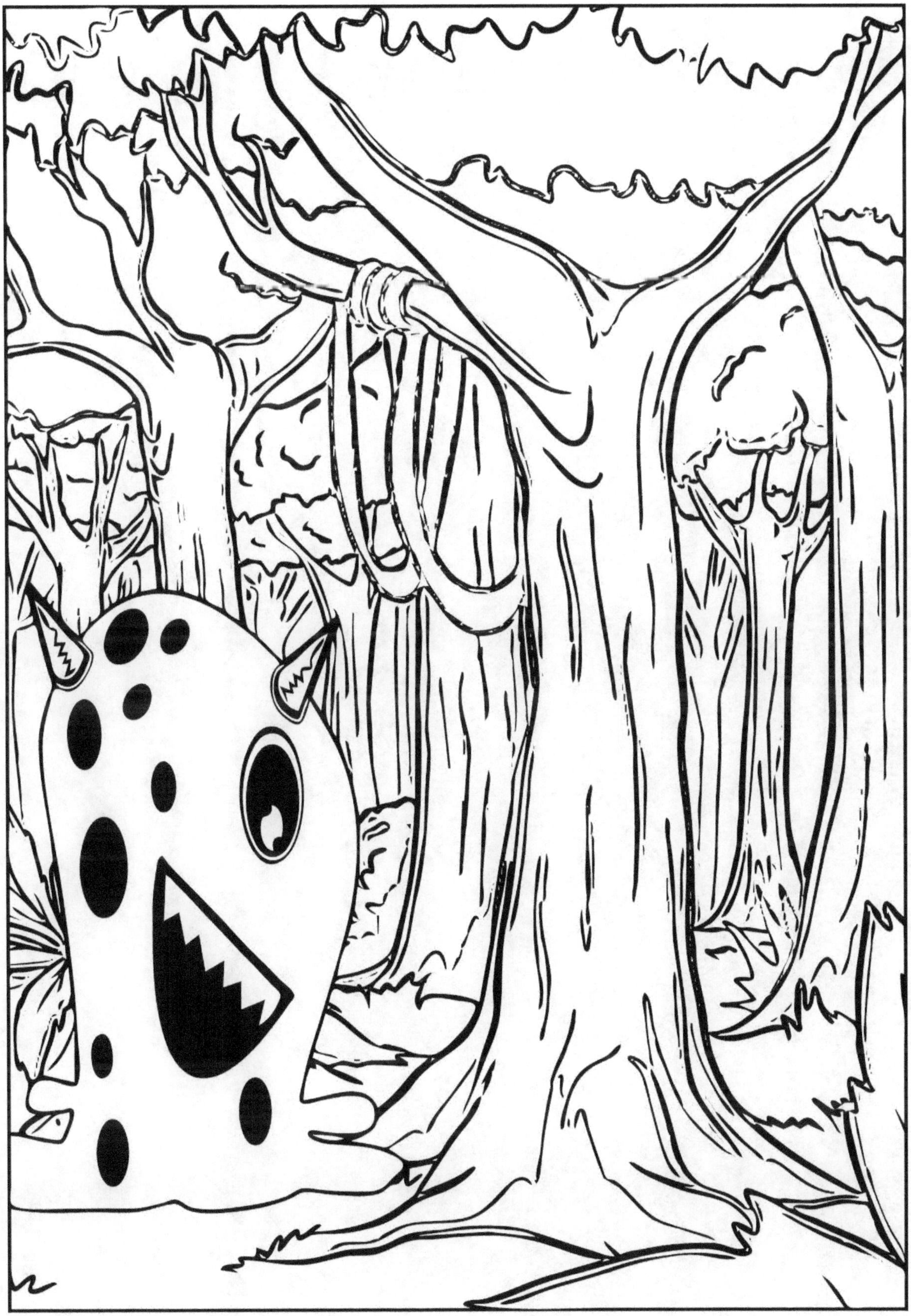

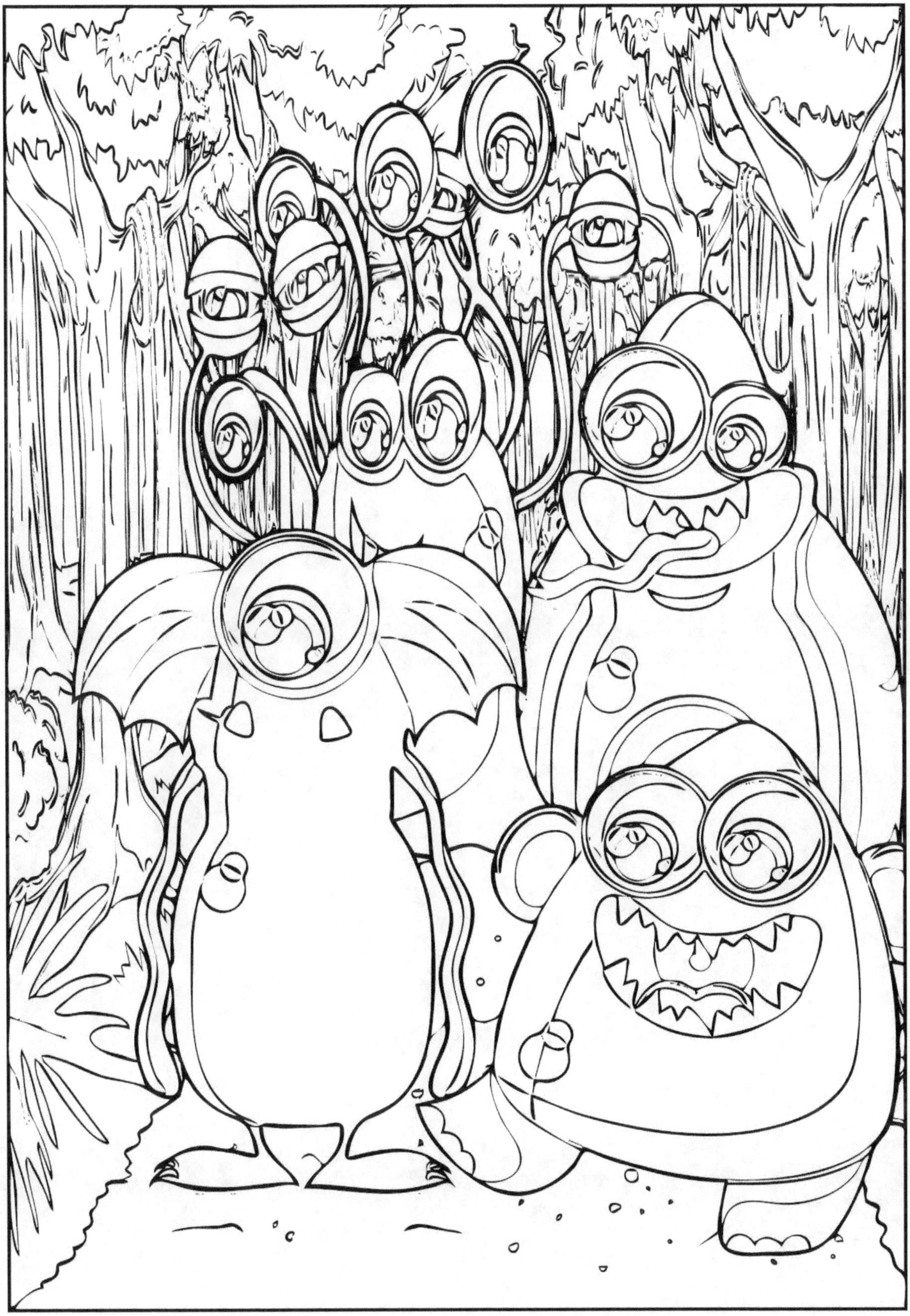

www.ingramcontent.com/pod-product-compliance
Lightning Source LLC
Chambersburg PA
CBHW080610180526
45168CB00007B/2852
* 9 7 8 1 5 1 7 2 9 9 9 4 1 *